New complet

W9-CCF-890

VENICE

Monuments, churches and museums

Edizioni KINA ITALIA

PREFACE

VENICE and its immensely rich artistic patrimony and the infinite reminders of its history written in the noble architecture of its palaces and churches and in all the different aspects of its particular urban fabric, are so rich and multiform a reality that it is impossible to condense such an exhaustive collection into a few pages. The following itineraries are intended merely as a suggestion, a basis on which to plan different tours of the city, whose stages in most cases, are undoubtedly worthy of more extensive examination. It will however be worth while following these itineraries with the help of a map of the city and of the wide selection of pictures which this guide offers and which, while giving an idea of the extraordinary variety of Venice's artistic treasures, also allows one to imagine the history of its splendid civilization.

Born as a place of refuge for the people of the Veneto Region from the Barbarian invasions of the V and VI Centuries, Venice responded in every way to their need of a place of rèfuge and seclusion. The varied and continually changing morphology of the lagoon, which at first sight appeared inhospitable and unreliable, was the saving of the fugitives. But also it soon became a stronghold for the new population, which when they had overcome problems of defence, demonstrated a forthrightness unequalled among Mediterranean péoples.

The Venetians progressed from the control of the maritime trade on the Adriatic and East Mediterranean coasts, which was already well established in the IX Century, to the conquest of Constantinople in 1204 on the occasion of the Fourth Crusade under the dogate of Enrico Dandolo. They pushed on into Egypt, going beyond the confines of the then known world and into

China, bringing precious stones, silks, spices and other rare merchandise back to the European market.

In the XIV and XV Centuries they consolidated their power in the Mediterranean and in the European hinterland making their rich and politically stable Republic into a European capital open to a thousand cultural movements. The cosmopolitan character of Venice and its commercial and cultural position astride the two civilizations of East and West, together made it an exciting and desirable goal for artists and men of culture.

In spite of its political decline which began towards the second half of the XVI Century and was so dramatically confirmed, after a period of alternating fortunes, when it was defeated by the Austrians in 1797, Venice still preserves the urban appearance of its centuries of glory.

Architecture of Byzantine influence, Romanesque, Gothic, Renaissance and Classical architecture, and art collections of great richness and interest bear testimony to the one-time presence in Venice of artistic personalities of outstanding skill and dynamic cultural enterprise.

The threat of a progressive sinking of the city with respect to the level of the sea is not discussed here but it is certainly known and feared by many who visit Venice every day. The signs of this disturbing phenomenon along with that of pollution, can often be seen close to the most beautiful of these urban jewels. And they will certainly be noticed on the itineraries which we suggest, side by side with the splendid architecture illustrated in the guide. If a knowledge of Venice can contribute, as we believe it can, to spreading a love for it and an interest in its destiny, even this guide will have contributed to the commitment of all those who seek to save it.

Index to the chapters

5

1 Itinerary

1 DEGLI SCALZI BRIDGE - 2 VENDRAMIN CALERGI PALACE - 3 PESARO PALACE (International Gallery of Modern Art and Oriental Museum) - 4 HOUSEOF GOLD (Franchetti Gallery) - 5 RIALTO BRIDGE - 6 FOSCARI PALACE - 7 GRASSI PALACE - 8 REZZONICO PALACE (Museum of 18th Century Venice) - 9 ACCADEMIA BRIDGE (and Gallery) - 10 DELLA SALUTE CHURCH - 11 ST. MARK'S BASILICA - 12 DOGE'S PALACE.

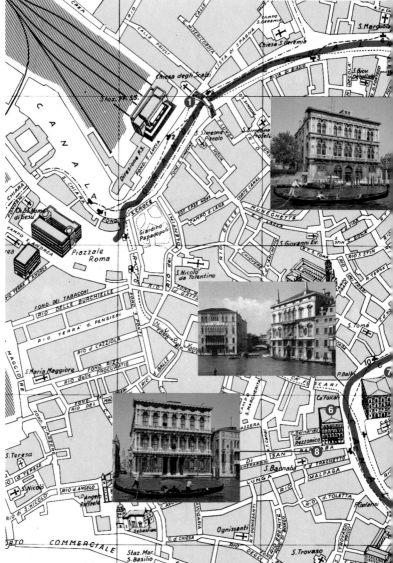

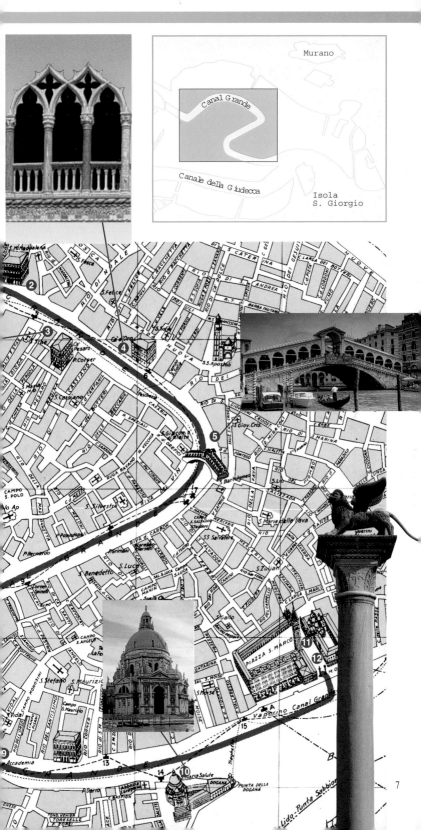

Murano

Canal Grande

Canale della Giudecca

Isola
S. Giorgio

7

Having arrived in Venice and left the last ramifications of the mainland traffic behind, at Piazzale Roma or at the S. Lucia Railway Station, the visitor is greeted with the most eloquent pictures of the city's «amphibious» character: the Grand Canal, busy with the coming and going of motorboats and gondolas and animated by hurrying life along its banks, reflects and multiplies the colours of the palaces overlooking it into a thousand twinkling fragments on the surface of the water. Colours and sounds mixed with the salty smell of the sea, give the first unforgettable impression of a unique urban environment where everyday life on the 400 bridges and 120 islands on which Venice is built, is continually swayed by the relationship between land and sea. The Grand Canal which with its sinuous path divides Venice in two, is the most spectacular artery for traffic in the city. In all probability the Canal, which is almost four kilometres long, was originally a river and played a role of primary importance from the earliest days of the Venice Republic. On its waters, precious merchandise arrived in Venice from the Orient, and along its banks numerous deposits or «fondaci» were situated and rented by the State to foreign merchants who stored their goods there and also resided there themselves when convenient. Rich Venetian merchants and nobles also built their residences beside the waters of the Grand Canal, vying

1

1) VENICE: aerial view of the city with S. Lucia railway station, the Grand Canal and Ponte degli Scalzi, which connects the two shores.

2) Ponte degli Scalzi

3) Chiesa degli Scalzi

2

8

with each other for luxury and elegance. They were generally built to a common design with a porch on the ground floor opening on to the water for the boats to tie up; one or two «noble floors» for habitation and commercial activities, and the upper floors for staff lodgings.

The palaces which nowadays overlook the Canal with a series of different but always architecturally elegant buildings, bear witness to the artistic and historic development of Venice. All the history of Venice, the Serenissima (or Most Serene), of its role as a maritime power, of its extraordinary economic power, and its artistic production, is written along the banks of the Grand Canal.

Thus this itinerary which follows the Canal as far as St. Mark's Basin is rich in interest. Whether one takes the steamboat from the landing stage in front of the railway station or prefers to rely on the gentle motion of a gondola, it is possible to enjoy the slow drifting by of an evocative and multicoloured scenario.

The first example of architecture of a certain importance which comes within sight of the visitor coming from the direction of the railway station or Piazzale Roma, is the Church of **SAN SIMEONE PICCOLO**, an imposing building on the edge of the Grand Canal. Built in the 18th century by Giovanni Scalfaretto, the church stands, with its high dome and impressive flight of steps up to the entrance, on the right bank of the Canal. It goes back to the IX Century. Not far away, the first of the three bridges over the Grand Canal can be seen in all the elegance of its beautiful design: the **DEGLI SCALZI BRIDGE** (Bridge of the Barefooted). Built in 1934 to a design by Eugenio Miozzi, the bridge, in white Istrian stone, is slender and delicate and the perfect connecting link between the Church of San Simeone Piccolo and the **DEGLI SCALZI CHURCH** (Church of the Barefooted) or of ST. MARY OF NAZARETH on the left bank. Built for the Barefooted Carmelites by Baldassare Longhena in 1670 to 1680, the church has a fine Baroque façade by G. Sardi.

3

9

Crossing the bridge, still on the left, one sees the single order façade of the **CHURCH OF ST. JEREMIAH** (San Geremia) which goes back to the XIII Century, was rebuilt and modified in the XVIII Century and in the XIX Century until it acquired its present, somewhat composite appearance. Next to the church, the **LABIA PALACE** (Palazzo Labia) is a sumptuous example of an eighteenth century habitation which contains numerous excellent frescoes by G. T. Tiepolo. The harmonious façade in Istrian stone is the work af Andrea Cominelli. Today the palace is the headquarters of the R.A.I. (Italian Broadcasting Corporation).

Proceeding along the waters of the Grand Canal between rows of palaces which overlook it from both sides and include the **Foscari Palace** of the XV Century, the **Gritti Palace** and the **Corner Palace** of the XVI Century, one arrives in front of the TURKISH WAREHOUSE (Fondaco dei Turchi) on the right bank of the Canal, a typical sign of that busy commercial activity which opened up trade between Venice and the East and made the Grand Canal into a cosmopolitan market place. A short distance away on the left, stands one of the most beautiful palaces in Venice: **VENDRAMIN CALERGI PALACE**, previously called Loredan. This splendid Renaissance palace where Richard Wagner died in 1883, was designed by Mauro Codussi who be-

1) The Grand Canal: Palazzo Labia and S. Jeremiah's Church

2) Fondaco dei Turchi

3) Palazzo Corner della Ca' Grande

4) Palazzo Vendramin Calergi

1

gan its construction in 1504. It was finished by the Lombardo's. As usual an entrance porch faces the Grand Canal. The very fine façade has loggias on two floors and two-light windows set in wide arches of simple and elegant design. Nothing remains unfortunately, of the frescoes by Giorgione and perhaps Titian which were inside, but nevertheless the palace, which is now occupied by the *City Casino*, is considered a masterpiece of Venetian Renaissance architecture.

Continuing along the course of the Grand Canal, the scenario of magnificent and multicoloured façades gradually unfolds.

First there are the high balconies of the

seventeenth century *Belloni Battigia Palace* which open on the right bank of the Grand Canal; then the gothic embroidery of the lovely five-light windows of *Erizzo alla Maddalena Palace* on the left; the elegant Renaissance *Tron Palace* which appears, still on the right, with its four-light windows; then the white façade of the *Church of San Stae followed almost immediately by that superb edifice, the* **PESARO PALACE**. The Pesaro Palace is considered a masterpiece of civic architecture by Baldassare Longhena who, in 1652, began the construction which was finished by Antonio Gaspari. It now houses the *Oriental Museum*, the *International Gallery of Modern Art*, and the famous *Biennial Festivals of Venice*. The Oriental Museum possesses an important patrimony of paintings, sculptures, ivories, lacquerware and costumes of the Far East.

In addition to the many examples of Venetian painting of the 19th and 20th centuries, the International Gallery of Modern Art also contains some noteworthy specimens of Italian and European

1) Ca' d'Oro: detail

3) Ca' Pesaro

2-4) Ca' d'Oro: façade

12

painting: from Hayez to Fattori, Signorini, De Chirico, Casorati, Boccioni and Rosai to Matisse and Chagall, Max Ernst, Tobey, Klee and Kandinsky.

The palace, which rises above a massive plinth, has an ashlar base in which there are two large doorways decorated with masks and various ornaments. The two upper floors with high windows separated by columns and decorated with plastic elements reveal the Sansovinian inspiration behind Longhena's design. Situated on the left bank at a short distance

1) Ca' d'Oro: detail of façade

2) Ca' d'Oro

1

from the Pesaro Palace on the Grand Canal, is the **HOUSE OF GOLD**, the Ca' d'Oro, Built in the first half of the 15th century for Marino Contarini, the Ca' d'Oro is an illustrious example of the decorated Gothic style which was becoming diffused in Venice at that time. After dilapidations caused by weather and a number of inadequate restorations nothing, unfortunately, remains of the gilding of the ornamental parts of the façade which gave the Ca' d'Oro its name of House of Gold. However, in spite of all

1-2) Views of the Rialto Bridge on the Grand Canal

3) The Grand Canal and the Rialto Bridge. The Regata Storica

this, the palace still has a rare elegance. While the right hand side of the façade has a large area of blank wall, on the left the play of plain wall and open tracery has the beauty of a piece of Gothic embroidery. A portico of pointed arches opens on to the Grand Canal on ground level while two Loggias on the upper floors open outwards with hexagonal windows with interlaced arches is an elaborate and immensely attractive design. Single windows and small balconies on the right wing repeat the Gothic design of the loggias on the left, so maintaining a style similar to that of the façade decorated with polychrome marbles and embellished with fascie and cornices of Byzantine influence. Today the House of Gold houses the FRANCHETTI GALLERY which takes its name from the last owner of the famous palace, Baron Giorgio Franchetti. The Gallery has a prestigious collection of paintings, bronzes, marbles and Venetian and foreign works of art of the 16th, 17th and 18th centuries.

After the House of Gold, still on the left bank, the CA' DA MOSTO Palace is typical of Veneto-Byzantine architecture. The Grand Canal then rounds a bend to reveal the imposing and majestic **RIALTO BRIDGE**. The quiet formal

1-2-3) Before the huge boat race in which gondoliers row small, twin-oar gondolas called gondolini, the Regata Storica is held on the Grand Canal.

elegance of the fine palaces is interrupted momentarily and the Grand Canal rediscovers the ancient animation of markets and shops.

The Rialto Bridge, a 16th century stone construction by Antonio da Ponte, is crossed by three flights of steps and under the double porticos shelters shops which face on to the wide steps which cross the centre of the bridge. There are numerous shops also in the adjoining lanes (calli) which, with the fish and vegetable stalls of the market, make the Rialto Bridge an important trading centre for the various products peculiar to Venice: from blown glassware to trinkets and jewellery; embroidery; lace from Burano; and antiques. A particularly spectacular view of the Canal, especially down it, can be seen from the flights of steps over the sides of the bridge. It is not surprising that the picture of the Rialto Bridge, where the beauty of Venice merges with its own pulsating activity, is among the most worthy of note in the lagoon city. On the first Sunday in September, the brilliant and spectacular race between gondolas participating in the famous *Historic Regatta* on the waters of the Grand Canal, passes under the Rialto Bridge. The gondola, the most traditional of Venetian craft, is seen on that occasion in large and sumptuous versions: the «bissone» in fact, which glide over the water rowed by oarsmen in eighteenth century costume, are like gigantic gondolas. Decorated with sea-gods, syrens, sea-horses, embroidered drapery and fringes, for that one day they restore Venice to the fascination and magnificence of its glorious past.

For one day the beautiful Venetian churches and palaces are seen against the historic background and atmosphere of centuries ago.

Following the course of the Grand Canal, further interesting discoveries are to be found on its banks. On the left bank, *Loredan Palace* and *Farsetti Palace*, now the Town Hall, are two examples of Veneto-Byzantine construction of the XIII and XII Centuries respectively. Still on the left, the Renaissance period GRIMANI PALACE is considered to be Sammicheli's masterpiece, while the *Corner Spinelli Palace* which is also Renaissance, is a magnificent work by Mauro Codussi. On the right, at the beginning of the last wide curve of the Canal stands the FOSCARI PALACE (Ca' Foscari), seat of the University Faculties of Economics and Commerce and of Foreign Languages and Literature. The splendid Venetian Gothic construction, richly decorated in marble, goes back to the first half of the 15th century.

Above the ground floor with its arches and simple windows opening on to the Canal, both the second and third floors have eight-arched loggias of fine Gothic design. Above the more elaborate loggia on the second floor, a wide fascia of white marble is decorated with the emblem of the Foscari family and ornamentation in bas-relief. Also the arches on the top floor, in white marble, have an elegant design which completes the beauty of the façade.

At a little distance from the Ca' Foscari, on the left bank, the **GRASSI PALACE** is the most important eighteenth century building in Venice, the work of Giorgio Massari.

The property of the rich patrician, Grassi family, the Palace is now the *International Art and Costume Centre.*

In the interior, a grandiose courtyard with an Ionic colonnade, now a covered hall, gives access to an elegant and formal staircase decorated with frescoes of

1

uncertain attribution (Longhi perhaps or Morlaiter), which depict festive scenes with personalities of the eighteenth century world. The external façade has a high ashlar base up to the height of two floors, and two upper floors which open on to the Grand Canal with high windows and balconies.

Almost opposite the Grassi Palace, on the right bank, a magnificent example of seventeenth century architecture is the **CA' REZZONICO** (or Casa, Venetian dialect for House, Rezzonico) which was begun by Baldassare Longhena in about 1660 and completed by G. Massari in 1745. Above the ashlar work of the ground floor, it is worth noting the richly ornamented first floor which opens on to the Grand Canal with large windows and balconies separated by Ionic semicolumns, with arches supported on columns and decorated with cherubs.

The second floor is more formal. The Palace houses the EIGHTEENTH CENTURY VENICE MUSEUM (Museo del Settecento Veneziano) and contains a collection of important works by G. B.

1) Ca' Rezzonico: ballroom with frescoes by Crosato

2) View of Ca' Rezzonico from the Grand Canal

2

3) Ca' Rezzonico: chandelier in the Brustolon room

Tiepolo, Rosalba Carriera, Guardi, Pietro Longhi and Canaletto in addition to a rich patrimony of ceramics, lacquerware, Murano glassware, and cloth: a rich and composite picture of one of the happiest centuries for Venetian art and at the same time an important cultural testimony. Continuing along the Grand Canal and passing, on the left, the picturesque *Falier Palace*, an ogival building, the **ACCADEMIA BRIDGE**, comes into view. This is the last of the three bridges which connect the two banks of the Canal. Built as a single arch in wood, the bridge takes its name from the nearby Academy of Fine Arts (Accademia delle Belle Arti) which houses in its Galleries an important patrimony of Venetian paintings of the period from the 14th to the 18th century. They include some interesting works by Veronese, Carpaccio, Giorgione, Titian, and numerous other illustrious artists. A short distance from the Accademia Bridge, on the left bank, there is the most interesting ogival construction of the XV Century *FRANCHETTI PALACE* (previously Cavalli).

1) The Basilica of S. Maria della Salute to the sunset

2) Detail of the Basilica, seen from above

3) General view of the floor

4) The interior of the Basilica

The Archduke Frederick of Austria died there in 1836. After it became the property of Baron Franchetti it was restored and modified by Camillo Boito in 1890. Now the Grand Canal gradually begins to widen. First of all, on the right, will be the majestic mass of Della Salute Church (Basilica della Salute or Basilica of Health) with its impressive roofs, to announce the opening of the prospect to wider views. Then the sinuous course of the Canal widens and comes out to an expansive marine horizon. We are in ST. MARK'S BASIN (Bacino di S. Marco). Here the splendour of the Doges' Palace (Palazzo Ducale) and the Byzantine domes of St. Mark's Basilica suddenly appear on the left and with unexpected magnificence complete the already glori-

4

ous scenario of the banks of the Grand Canal.

The **DELLA SALUTE CHURCH**, which with its great white mass represents a jump in size with respect to the other buildings in the vicinity, is the work of Baldassare Longhena. Taking his inspiration from the buildings on a central plan, typical of the architecture of Bramante and Palladio, he built the church to an octagonal plan culminating in an enormous semispherical dome flanked, at a later date, by a second dome of smaller dimensions over the presbitery. A polygonal flight of stone steps, imposing

1) **Basilica della Salute. Cain and Abel (Titian)**

2) **The Madonna della Salute, known as Mesopanditissa**

3) **S. Jerome (Titian)**

4) **S. Augustine (Titian)**

5) **S. John the Evangelist (Titian)**

6-7) **Praying Madonna (G.B. Salvi)**

8) **David and Goliath (Titian)**

9) **The Marriage of Cana (Tintoretto)**

1

3

2

4

5

and formal, leads to the entrance doorway in the central façade which opens with a great oak door faced with bronzed copper panels. Three lateral façades correspond to six chapels surrounding the central space in the interior. The façade, the numerous statues of angels, saints and Marian figures of the Old Testament are all realized in white stone.

Fifteen modillions or corbels in concentric strata which emphasize the lines of the dome are carved in the same stone.

A Madonna and Child above the gable at the entrance represents the central point

1) S. Mark's Basilica: the façade

2) Aerial view of S. Mark's Square

3) The Lion of S. Mark

4) Clock with the signs of the zodiac

5) S. Mark's Square. Clock tower and chariot horses

of the iconographical theme which dominates the whole church both inside and out - the glorification of the Virgin. The church was in fact built as a votive offering made to the Madonna in 1630 begging her to free the city from the terrible pestilence which afflicted the people in that year. That is why every one of the six chapels which open towards the centre of the church, except for an altar dedicated to St. Anthony, is dedicated to a mistery of the Virgin. A symbolic reference to the Marian rosary is constituted by a ring of thirty roses which marks the centre of the splendid mosaic floor in polychrome marble. The luminosity of the church emphasizes the glorious chromatic effects in the floor with its geometrical designs in concentric circles. The High Altar, in octagonal shape, is ornamented with statues in

4

5

29

1) S. Mark's Basilica.
S. Clement's Door
(11th century)
2) The interior of S.
Mark's Basilica seen
from the nave, with
the Byzantine cross
hanging from the
Pentecost dome
3) The Four Moors
4-5) Details of floors
6) Lunette in the San
Alipio Door: mosaic
portraying the remo-
val of S. Mark's
body to the Basilica.
7) Detail of the 13th-
century atrium:
Noah releasing the
dove from the Ark
after the flood

marble which depict scenes of the driving out of the plague. The image of the Madonna of Good Health in the centre came from the Cathedral of Candia and was placed here in 1670.

In addition to a number of fine altarpieces by Luca Giordano, Pietro Liberi, and Titian, the Basilica possesses a considerable patrimony of works of art from the Island of Santo Spirito: twelve works by Titian, others by Palma the Younger, Padovanino and the famous painting by Tintoretto depicting the Marriage of Cana.

On St. Mark's Basin to the left, appears what might be called the heart of Venice. Centre of the religious and political life of the Most Serene Republic, St. Mark's Basilica and the Doges' Palace constitute, in spite of their obvious dissimilarity of style, an architectural entity, complex and yet compact whitin the geometrical prospect of St. Mark's Square and the Piazzetta which overlooks the sea.

ST. MARKS (San Marco) is a church with a wealth of history behind it, a fantastic and multiform coagulation of different styles, proof of Venice's close associations with the East and of its character as a city - a bridge between the cultures of East and West. Its structure which has no precedent in the history of our peninsula, is presumably due to the project of some unknown Greek architect. Its *plan* is that of a Greek cross with four domes on the arms and a fifth in the centre.

It was only in 1063, during the Contarini dogate, that the building of the Basilica

in its present form was begun.

Previously, in 829, under the dogate of Giustiniano Partecipazio, work was begun on a temple on the site of the present Basilica, to house the remains of St. Mark which had been brought back from the Mohammedans of Alexandria in Egypt the year before. It is supposed that the Temple, which was consacrated in 832 was in the traditional form of Paleochristian temples, composed of a nave and two aisles, one or three apses with the relative crypts, a portico in front and probably frescoed decorations. It marked the fulfilment of a prophesy and the crowning of a dream dear to all Venetians. In fact, according to tradition, when the Evangelist St. Mark arrived at the islands in the lagoon, he dreamt of an Angel who said to him. «Here you will find peace, Mark, my evangelist». Thus the construction of the Basilica was the accomplishment of a spiritual duty and at the same time a motive for exhaltation and the collective identification with the destiny of Venice. Unfortunately the Basilica was destroyed by fire in 976 but was rebuilt immediately afterwards. Eventually the building of the present church which substituted the second, coincided with a moment of great prosperity for the Republic, and with the legitimate desire of the Venetian people to express its greatness with a *Ducal Chapel* (Cappella Ducale). This in fact was the destination of the Basilica: the Ducal Chapel, site of the ritual celebrations of all the major events in the history of the Republic until 1807, when finally it became the Cathedral of Venice.

Its architecture and the rich decorations for which it is famous, recount its history via the various expressions of a creativity both multiform and fortunate. Centuries of art and generations of unknown and famous artists each of whom played a part, with modifications and additions until the 15th century, have left evidence of the most varied styles, from Byzantine to Romanesque, Gothic and Renaissance. The result, with miraculous cohesion, has the beauty of the finest choral

1) S. Mark's Basilica. Salome's dance: detail

2) Iconostasis: 14th-century Gothic structure

3) Mosaics in the atrium: the Genesis dome

singing in which the refinement of the most cultured arts merges serenely with the most ingenuous expressions of popular phantasy.

Some of the materials which had been used in the previous Basilica – door posts and window frames, capitals, transennae – were used again for the same purpose; others were set into the walls of the new Basilica. Marbles of every kind and colour were brought from distant lands, 500 columns of every style, Romanesque bas-reliefs; Gothic, Romanesque and Byzantine capitals: every prize from conquests, discoveries, creations, found a place in St. Mark's as if the spaces in the church were pages of a collective diary.

The façade of the church whose splendour overlooks the beautiful St. Mark's Square, consists of two orders of arches, five at the bottom set farther forward, and five above. Groups of multicoloured marble columns separate the lower arches which enclose five fine doorways. On each of these excellent bas-reliefs depict episodes in religious history or elements describing normal daily life. One notes, for example, the *Portal of St. Alipio* with pictures of the Epiphany, of Christ and the Apostles and the Marriage of Cana; and the third portal on which are depicted the principal *trades* or *professions* followed in Venice. The five upper arches, decorated with mosaic work and surmounted by a decoration in decorated Gothic style consisting of statues, foliage and cusps, make the backcloth for a narrow terrace. The central arch, wider than the others as in the case of the corresponding one below, is closed by a làrge glass window from which the interior of the Basilica receives light and which serves as a background for the *four celebrated bronze horses.*

This magnificent example of Greek-Alexandrine art of uncertain attribution, was the prize taken after the victorious battle against Constantinople in 1204. On the peak of the cusp at the top of the central arch, the statue of *St. Mark* with angels reaching towards it on either side,

is the work of Nicolò Lamberti. Lower down, against a blue background studded with golden stars, stands the *Lion of St. Mark*, the emblem of Venice which is also represented on the nearby clock tower. The five famous domes of St. Mark's are topped by five Oriental style lanterns on which shine the crosses with crossed arms.

With the splendid beauty of its mosaics, the atrium which gives access to the Basilica, gives a foretaste of the decorative elements which also pevail in the interior, and of the sacred theme of all the mosaic decorations. These mosaics, which represent the Biblical stories of the *Creation* and the *Flight out of Egypt*,

1) S. Mark's Basilica. Reliquary containing S. George's arm

2) The Pala d'Oro (Gold Altarpiece)

were executed by Venetian artists of the XIII Century.

The Interior of the Basilica, evocative and interesting as it is, is a long succession of domes and arches, a true and worthy casket which contains a wealth of precious treasures. Of them all we shall mention the *Gold Altarscreen* which glows behind the High Altar where the relics of St. Mark are kept. The screen, which is among the most precious works of gold and jewels in existence, is studded with with gems and enamels and is composed of some parts which are datable from the X to the XIV Century.

But the reason for which St. Mark's is called the Basilica of gold and which

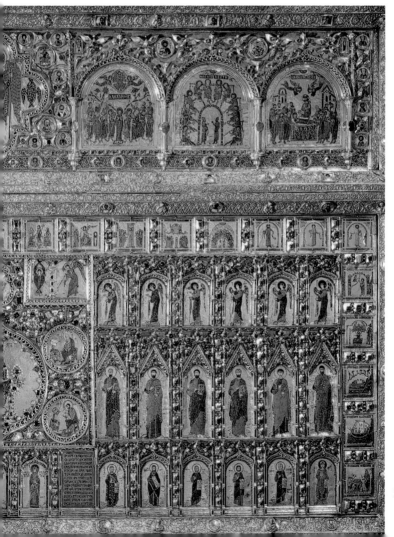

makes it particularly magnificent, is the
glorious mosaic mantle which covers the
vaulted roof for a total surface of over
4000 metres. This extraordinary and yet
anonymous work of art was begun perhaps around 1070 when the apse was decorated with representations of the four
evangelists. This art of Byzantine and
Ravennate origin, found in Venice a richly fertile soil for its finest expression,
thanks also to the already well developed
glass craftsmanship. The splendid colours of the glass tiles used on a background of tiles faced with gold leaf acquired brilliance and expressiveness.
The theme of the great mosaic composi-
tion, presumably inspired by the decorative plan of the Basilica of the Saints
Apostles in Constantinople, seems to be
unique: the connecting thread is the glorification of the Church of Christ, realized in the dome above the presbytery,
in the central dome, and in that towards

1) S. Mark's Basilica: 3rd-century sardonyx ampulla

2) S. Michael the Archangel, saints and precious stones

3) Detail of chariot

the entrance. In those the mosaics depict respectively *The Church Anticipated by the Prophets, The Church Living in Christ, The Church Actuated through Preaching. The Triumph of the Church in the Last Judgement* is seen in the large arch above the entrance. Next to these decorations which represent the principal subjects of the cycle, other mosaics portray episodes in the religious life of Venice, such as the story of St. Mark. Thus the Biblical stories represented in the external atrium are a preview of the sacred themes developed in the interior and constitute an element of continuity in the stylistic variations in the Basilica.

The famous CLOCK TOWER (Torre dell'Orologio) stands near St. Mark's Basilica on the North side of the square. This Renaissance construction by Mauro Codussi is raised on a wide arcade with three square sections one above the other. In the first, a large clock face indicates the hours, the phases of the moon and the movement of the sun in the various signs of the zodiac depicted in gold on a background of blue enamel. In the second section, a Madonna and

Child attributed to A. Leopardi, is placed in an aedicule. On each side of the Madonna two windows show the hours. On the third floor of the tower, the *Lion* of St. Mark, gilded like that on the Basilica. On the terrace on the top of the tower are the famous bronze statues of *Moors* striking the hours with hammers on a large bell.

The **DUCAL PALACE** or PALACE OF THE DOGES (Palazzo Ducale o Palazzo dei Doge) which faces on to the smaller square, the Piazzetta next to St. Mark's Square and towards the quay in St. Mark's Basin, is the largest civic building in Venice, theatre of all the political history of the Republic and location of an artistic patrimony of the highest order represented by numerous paintings of the Venetian school. It appears, to anyone arriving by the Grand Canal, in all the splendour of its two principal façades decorated with a geometrical lozenge design in white, grey and red marbles, with

1) The Doge's Palace. The "Mouth of Truth"
2-5-6) Views of the façade of the Doge's Palace
3) Capital with winged lion
4) Capital with statue of S. Theodore, the first patron saint of Venice

a wonderful chromatic effect. It was the
seat of the Doge and the High Magistrature of the Republic, then of Govern-
nment Offices and cultural bodies. Its
construction began around 1300 to re-
place the old battlemented castle built in
the distant past, 814, and destroyed by
fires in 976 and in 1105. Architects and
artists such as the Dalle Masegne family,
Pietro Lamberti, Antonio Rizzo, P. Lombardo, G. Spavento, Scarpagnino and
many others looked after the various
phases of the work. The two principal façades which, as mentioned above, overlook the quay and the Piazzetta are pre-
sented in three orders. On the ground
floor, an arcade with wide pointed
arches; on this an open loggia with inflected arches, two for each arch on the
level below, with elegant Gothic quatre-
foil tracery; the upper part with ogee and
round windows in a blank wall is decorated, as we have said, with a geometrical
design in polychrome marbles and ends
with a white Veneto-Byzantine crenella-
tion which recalls the embroidery-like
vaults of the porticoes and of the gallery

1) The Doge's Palace.
Courtyard

2) Detail of 16th-
century façade with
two tiers of loggias

3) The Golden Staircase

4) Assembly Room

below. Access to the courtyard of the Palace is through the main entrance – the elegantly majestic *Door of the Papers* (Porta della Carta), the work of G. and B. Bon. The courtyard is enclosed by the beautiful internal façade of the Palace which is richly decorated in Gothic, Renaissance and Classical style. On the North side of the courtyard one finds the *Foscari Portico and Arch* (Porticato e l'Arco Foscari) in Venetian Gothic style with Renaissance elements. In front of the Foscari Arch is the famous *Giants' Staircase* (Scala dei Giganti) by A. Rizzo, with statues of *Mars* and *Neptune* (Marte e Nettuno) by Sansovino. The *Clock Façade* (facciata dell'Orologio), the work of Monopola, rises above the Foscari portico.

The internal structure of the Palace has a certain complexity. From the *Censors'*

1) The Doge's Palace. Youth and Age - detail (Veronese)

2) The Bridge of Sighs

3) Rio della Canonica

Staircase (Scala dei Censori) one enters the *floor with the loggias* (piano delle logge) which open on to the inner courtyard along three sides and to the exterior on two façades. Facing the Piazzetta, the unusual beauty of the *Foscari Loggia*, added during the dogate of Francesco Foscari, is particularly noteworthy.

The two upper or noble floors are reached via the *Golden Staircase* (Scala d'Oro), a magnificent sixteenth century work designed by Sansovino and carried out by Scarpagnino. Reserved, in the old days, to the magistrates and officials of the Republic, the staircase goes to the first noble floor, seat of the High Magistrature and ancient residence of the Doge. The rooms on this floor, to mention a few, the *Hall of the Great Council, Hall of the Criminal Magistrates* and *Hall of the Magistrates at Law* were named according to the function of their inhabitants and still contain numerous works of art. It is interesting to note that these can still be found in the exact places for which they were originally intended, having been commissioned to decorate the walls and ceilings of particular rooms where they still remain enclosed in richly splendid frames. The Hall of the Great Council contains the great canvas of *Paradise* by Tintoretto and his son, and also

the fine work by Paolo Veronese representing the *Triumph of Venice*.

The Last Judgement by Palma the Younger can be seen in the Hall of the Scrutiny, while in the Hall of the Magistrates at Law the beautiful marble statues of *Adam* and *Eve* by A. Rizzo are certainly worthy of note. Finally, in the Doge's lodgings there are works by Carpaccio, Bellini, and among others, some interesting paintings by Bosch, the so-called «stregozzi» of satirical inspiration.

Continuing up the Golden Staircase, one comes to the second noble floor, this also divided into numerous rooms, the headquarters of various government bodies. In the Room of the Four Doors, we remember Titian's fine painting of *Doge Grimani Kneeling before the Faith*. In the Hall of the Anticollege, *Mercury and the Graces* and *Bacchus and Ariadne*, both by I. Tintoretto, and the *Rape of Europa* by Paolo Veronese. On the ceiling and walls of the *Senate Hall*, in magnificently carved frames are various works by Tintoretto, Palma the Younger, Marco Vecellio and Vicentino.

Not to be overlooked in concluding this visit to the beauties of St. Mark's Square, is the famous *Bridge of Sighs* (Ponte dei Sospiri), an important tourist landmark even though the ancient function of the bridge was a far from happy one: it connects the Hall of the Magistrates to the *New Prisons* and many an unhappy creature had reason to sigh as he crossed it.

2 Itinerary

1 ST. JULIAN - 2 ST. MARY FORMOSA - 3 ST. MARY OF THE MIRACLES - 4 ST. JOHN AND ST. PAUL (or ST. ZANIPOLO) - 5 ST. FRANCIS OF THE VINE - 6 DANDOLO PALACE (Danieli Hotel) - 7 ST. ZACHARIAH - 8 ARSENAL - 9 ST. PETER IN CASTELLO.

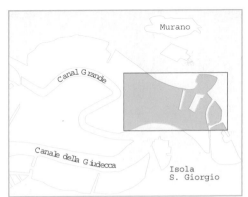

Murano

Canal Grande

Canale della Giudecca

Isola
S. Giorgio

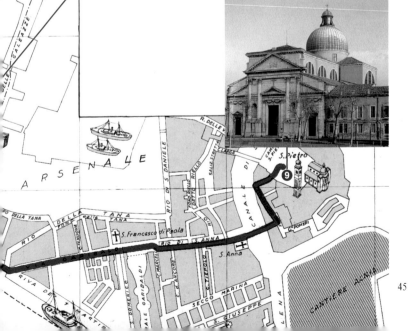

The first stop in the second itinerary will be the **CHURCH of ST. JULIAN** (S. Giuliano) in the little *square* or *campo* of the same name, laid out in 1553 by Sansovino and Vittoria there where the ancient church had stood since 829. The new project was financed by Tommaso Rangone, a doctor and scholar to whom Sansovino (or perhaps Vittoria) dedicated a beautiful statue in bronze which shows him seated and which can be seen above the portal in the centre of the façade with two orders of semicolumns.

The interior boasts some interesting works of art including the *Glory of St. Julian* by Palma the Younger, the *Miracle of St. Julian* and the *Martyrdom of St. Julian* both by Antonio Zanchi, the *Pietà* a high relief in marble by Girolamo Campagna and various other interesting works by the Venetian school.

Leaving the church and walking along the lanes (calli) of the Guerra district we arrive at the small canal – Rio di Santa Maria Formosa. On the little square or campo of the same name beside the canal, the **CHURCH OF SANTA MARIA FORMOSA** is surrounded by the beautiful façades of three palaces – *Ruzzini-Friuli*, *Donà* and *Vitturi Palaces*. The square, one of the loveliest in Venice, has in past centuries been the theatre of « bull festivals » and various other open-air entertainments. The church was rebuilt in 1492 by Mauro Codussi in the shape of a Latin cross. It has two façades in different styles, one of the seventeenth century which overlooks the square, the other in the style of Sansovino which overlooks the canal (Rio). An unusual bell-tower in Baroque style was built in 1688 to a design by the priest F. Zucconi. The dome, destroyed in the earthquake of 1688 and again in the bombing in 1916, was rebuilt in 1921. The harmonious and attractive interior of the church is, as we have said, in the form of a Latin cross with a nave and two aisles. Among the more outstanding works of art and worthy of special notice is the fine polyptych by Palmer the Elder, peinted around 1509, which depicts *St. Barbara* between *Sts. Sebastian and Anthony Abbot* and, in the upper order, *the Pietà between Saints Dominic and John the Baptist*. This work, which is of excellent quality and was painted by the artist when a young man, earned him fame equal to that of Giorgione and Titian. The triptych painted by Bartolomeo Vivarini in about 1473 depicting the *Nativity of Mary*, the *Madonna of Mercy*, and the *Meeting between St. James and St. Anne* is also worthy of note. According to tradition the Church of Santa Maria Formosa was erected in the VII Century by St. Magnus, Bishop of Oderzo, to whom the Virgin is said to have appeared as a splendid (formosa) matron. The church has been the seat of numerous schools of religion and crafts.

Proceeding from the church in the direction of the small canal Rio di S. Marina. we cross first the Rio del Paradiso which is the continuation of the lane or calle of the same name. The *Calle del Paradiso*, among the most picturesque in Venice, merits a stroll between its houses which have well preserved Byzantine and Gothic elements. At the beginning of the calle, crossing the BRIDGE OF PARADISE (Ponte del Paradiso), we pass under an elegant Gothic arch, the Arch of Paradise which has a frontispiece with perforated cusps and is decorated on both faces by a bas-relief of the Madonna of Mercy and the emblems of the Foscari and Mocenigo families.

Walking the short distance to the square – Campo di S. Marina and crossing the canal of the same name we shall pass the Van Axel Palace, better known as the PALAZZO SANUDO, and arrive at the CHURCH of ST. MARY OF THE MIRACLES (S. Maria dei Miracoli) with the rio dei Miracoli running beside it. Sanudo Palace, which is also called the Soranso Palace, is an interesting fifteenth century building with beautiful Gothic four-light windows decorated with Veneto-Byzantine elements on the two façades.

The Church of **ST. MARY OF THE MI-**

1) Rio San Giovanni Laterano

2) S. Maria dei Miracoli

3) Rio Van Axel

RACLES, a splendid and rare example of a Renaissance Church, was built between 1481 and 1489 by P. Lombardo and is considered one of his masterpieces. The façade is divided into two orders of pilaster strip, the first ending in an architrave, the second with arcades with two single-light windows between. A large lunette crowns the façade to correspond with the barrel vaulting in the interior. The elegant rectangular interior with a nave and no aisles, contains some precious works of art, paintings and sculptures by Palma the Younger, the Lombardo family, Vittoria, Campagna and others.

Not far away, the WIDMAN-FOSCARI Palace on the calle of the same name, was the residence of rich Corinthian merchants.

It has a beautiful seventeenth century façade and is richly ornamented with stuccoes inside.

Going now in the direction of the Rio dei Mendicanti, we come to one of the principal churches in Venice: the **BASILICA OF SAINTS JOHN AND PAUL**(S. Giovanni e Paolo), also known as SAN ZANIPOLO. This church, which is an outstanding example of Gothic religious architecture, is situated in the square of the same name next to the Renaissance Great School of St. Mark (Scuola Grande di S. Marco) now the Civic Hospital. De-

corated with simplicity and restraint, the red brick construction is strikingly effective next to the white marbles covering the façade of the School of St. Mark. The building which was begun in 1246 was not completed until a good two centuries later. From 1430, the year it was consecrated, the church was used for the entombment of doges and military leaders until today it is looked upon as the Pantheon of the Most Serene Republic. A simple cornice of ogee arches outlines the upper edge of the façade and continues along the sides. On the façade a second cornice of white stone, parallel with

5

51

the small arches motif, culminates in three aedicules which give character to the design of the façade. In the centre of this a large round window framed in white stone and two circular windows at the sides give light to the interior. The portal, a splendid example of the transitional style between Gothic and Renaissance, is surmounted by a large ogival arch supported at the sides by two groups of columns. Along the sides a series of round windows and long narrow two-light windows framed in white stone in contrast with the red brick. The interior, in the shape of a Latin cross, is harmonious and pleasing. The ogee arches and the walls of the nave and aisles are joined together by a series of wooden chains.

Funerary monuments, some of which are of extraordinary artistic interest, line the sides of the nave and aisles and the transepts. Among those along the right aisle, the Tomb of Doge Pietro Mocenigo by Pietro Lombardo (1485) is considered one of his masterpieces. On the left of the High Altar, the *Monument to Doge Andrea Vendramin* is a magnificent example of Venetian funerary art of the fifteenth century. This was executed by the Lombardo family except perhaps for the architectural part which some attribute to Leopardi.

In the left aisle there is a Renaissance

1-2) Basilica of SS. John and Paul. Interior of the Church

3-4) Polyptych by G. Bellini - details

5) Polyptych by G. Bellini

6) The glory of S. Dominic (G.B. Piazzetta)

3

4

5

6

Monument to Doge Pasquale Malipiero by Pietro Lombardo which should not be overlooked.

The most famous among the pictorial works is the splendid *Polyptych of St. Vincenzo Ferreri*, an early work by Bellini and masterpiece of the beginning of the Venetian Renaissance. In the Chapel of St. Dominic, the *Glory of St. Dominic* by G. B. Piazzetta (1727) is a masterpiece of eighteenth century Venetian work. Also Leandro Bassano's picture The *Approvation of the Dominican Order*, celebrates the Basilica's connection with the Dominican Order to which the land on which

1) Large Gothic window

2) The Approval of the Dominican Order (L. da Bassano)

it is built originally belonged. In the CHAPEL OF THE ROSARY, restored in 1913 after a terrible fire, a valuable collection of works of art, paintings and sculptures by such artists a Piazzetta, Veronese, Vittoria, Bonassa, Morlaiter and other reputable artists of the Venetian school is carefully preserved. Outside the church, the monument to Colleoni realized by Leopardi to a design by Verrocchio, is the perfect complement to the theme of the Glories of the Republic which decorates the interior.

Leaving the Basilica to follow the Calle S. Giovanni e Paolo, Calle Barbaria delle

Tole and Calle Del Caffetier, crossing Rio di Santa Giustina and passing the Church of St. Justina (S. Giustina), along the Calle di S. Francesco della Vigna, we reach the Church of the same name. The **CHURCH OF ST. FRANCIS OF THE VINEYARD** was built in 1543 by I. Sansovino on a vineyard which had been donated to the Franciscans by Marco Ziani. The façade with its classical lines was built to a model by Palladio in the second half of the sixteenth century. It contains some fine works by the Lombardo's, Santacroce, Bellini, Vivarini, etc.

From St. Francis of the Vineyard, going on foot towards St. Mark's Basin, it is possible to visit the Churches of *St. Lawrence* (San Lorenzo), *St. John of the Knights of Malta* (S. Giovanni dei Cavalieri di Malta), and *St. Antonin.*

St. Lawrence's (S. Lorenzo) on the large square or campo of the same name, is a very ancient church rebuilt in Baroque style by S. Sorella but never completed. The Church of St. John of the Knights of Malta contains an interesting Renaissance Altar and a beautiful cloister.

St. Antonin, in Campo S. Antonin, was rebuilt on the previous very ancient church, to a design attributed to Longhena.

Proceeding directly to the Riva degli Schiavoni or reaching it via the Doges' Palace and then along St. Mark's Basin, we arrive at the **DANDOLO PALACE,**

1) S. Francesco della Vigna

2) Palazzo Dandolo

3) S. Giovanni in Bragora

4) Cima da Conegliano: The Baptism of Jesus

now the DANIELI HOTEL, a fine XV Century construction with an ogival façade, loggias with intertwined arches, and balconies, the seat in the XVI Century of

the French Embassy.

The Churches of **ST. JOHN IN BRA-GORA** and **ST. ZACHARIAH** (S. Giovanni and S. Zaccaria) are close by. The former, in Campo Bandiera e Moro, goes back to the VIII Century and was restored in 1475. The façade is in late Venetian Gothic, the interior, with a nave and two aisles is harmonious and pleasing. It contains, among other works, an interesting picture by B. Vivarini, *The Madonna and Child enthroned and Sts. Andrew and John the Baptist*, (1478), and

1) S. Zacharias

2-3-4) Views of the Arsenal

a work by Alvise Vivarini, *Christ Risen* of 1498. The *Church of St. Zachariah* in the lovely homonimous square, was commissioned in the IX Century by the Doge G. Partecipazio and was rebuilt several times until it attained its present form which dates from the fifteenth century. The interesting façade, the result of two successive alterations, by Gambello and by Codussi, combines Gothic and Renaissance characteristics. Works by Tintoretto, Antonio Vivarini, Titian, Palma the Elder, and others are to be found inside.

From the Riva degli Schiavoni to the Fondamenta dell'Arsenale, along the Riva dell'Arsenale, we come to the **ARSENAL** (Arsenale) an unusual and grandiose complex of shipyards around the Great Dock (Grande Darsena). Founded in 1104 by Doge Ordelaffo Falier, and enlarged several times in later centuries, it was eventually equipped to look after the Bucintoro, the State barge of the Doges, and to produce ropes, weapons, explosives and modern warships. The land entrance on the left hand side of the canal is the earliest example of Renaissance architecture in Venice (1460). The Arsenal now contains an interesting **HISTORICAL NAVAL MUSEUM** in what used to be the granary of the Most Serene Re-

public. Leaving the Riva S. Biagio, then turning left in Via Garibaldi and proceeding along the Fondamenta S. Anna beside the Rio S. Anna, we come to the S. Pietro Canal. Across the canal the ISLAND OF ST. PETER (Isola di S. Pietro), inhabited by fishermen, was one of the first islands the Veneto fugitives settled on. It was known in the past as the Island of *Olivolo*, then of *Castello*, and is the site of the what was the Cathedral of Venice until 1807: the **CHURCH OF ST. PETER OF CASTELLO**. Not particularly remarkable from an architectural point of view, the church is rather more interesting historically. Built in the VIII Century in place of the pre-existing Church of Sts. Sergius and Bacchus (of 650), it was the subject of successive restorations until the XVII Century. The façade, in two orders, in Istrian stone, is the work of F. Smeraldi (1596) and was inspired, with not very brilliant results, by a Palladian design. The bell-tower, also in Istrian stone, is by Codussi. The Latin cross interior contains the relics of the first Patriarch of Venice St. Lorenzo Giustiniano (died in 1465), and works by such artists as Morlaiter, Padovanino, Luca Giordano, Ruschi. The sixteenth century ex Palace of the Patriarchs is located at a short distance from the church.

1-2-3) Basilica with the Cathedral of S. Pietro di Castello. Façade, interior and Adoration of the Magi (P. Ricchi)

3 Itinerary

1 DELLE GUGLIE BRIDGE (Cannaregio) - **2** St. JOB'S CHURCH - **3** THE SYNAGOGUE or SCHOLA GRANDE (?) - **4** ST. ALVISE CHURCH - **5** CHURCH OF THE MADONNA OF THE GARDEN - **6** ABBEY OF MERCY - **7** SANTA FOSCA CHURCH - **8** ST. SOPHIE'S - **9** SAINTS APOSTLES - **10** ST. JOHN CHYSOSTOM - **11** CHURCH OF THE JESUITS

The third itinerary, starting from the *Delle Guglie Bridge* (Ponte), includes a visit to St. Job's Church near the canal, Rio S. Giobbe (St. Job) which can be reached by following the bank of the Cannaregio Canal. Thus, all the way from the Dalle Guglie Bridge it is an itinerary almost entirely of the discovery of beautiful churches, some in delightfully solitary places.

The **DELLE GUGLIE BRIDGE**, a fine stone construction which goes back to 1580, is situated at the beginning of the Cannaregio Canal which is the second internal waterway in the city after the

1) Ponte delle Guglie and Canale di Cannaregio

Grand Canal. The name of the bridge comes from the four obelisks (guglie) which stand at the ends. It was restored in 1776.

The *three arched bridge* (ponte dei tre archi) built by Tirali in 1688 and restored in 1794, crosses the Cannaregio Canal just before it debouches into the lagoon. **St. Job's Church** stands a short distance away. Built to the order of Doge Cristoforo Moro in honour of the Saint who had predicted his dogate, the church was begun in 1450 by A. Gambello in Gothic style and eventually completed in Renaissance form by F. Lombardo and con-

sacrated in 1493. Recent restorations have brought some of the first stylistic elements back to light. The façade, with extremely simple lines, is opened by a splendid portal with pilaster strip in Lombard style, possibly executed by G. Bergamasco, and surmounted by statues of *Saints Anthony and Ludovick the Bishop and St. Bernard.*

A bas-relief in the lunette above the portal represents St. Job and St. Francis of Assisi. The remaining wing of the *cloister* in fourteenth century style, and a *well curb* are in the square on the right side of the church. The church, which has a nave only and cross vaulting, contains some quite valuable works of art. The more memorable ones are the *Nativity* by G. Savoldo (1540) at the altar of the Gothic Contarini Chapel which is believed to be all that remains of the fourteenth century oratory; *The Virgin Mary between Saints Michael and Anthony*, a triptych by Antonio Vivarini and Giovanni d'Alemagna; and in the paving of the presbitery, *the tombstone of Doge Cristoforo Moro and his wife, a masterpiece of Lombardesque art.*

Taking up the itinerary again at the Delle Guglie Bridge we shall find ourselves in the ghetto. Since 1527, by disposition of the Governors of the City, the ghetto has contained the houses of the Jewish people, and so also the synagogues or schole where they celebrated the rites of their religion. In the square called

1) Ponte dei tre Archi

2) The Ghetto

3) Church of S. Job. The Nativity (C. Savoldo)

Campo Ghetto Nuovo (or New Ghetto) the **GRAND SCHOLA** (1526) of German rites, is also a small museum: it contains, in fact, some precious tapestries, sacred vestments, and objects of the cult. The *Italian Schola*, on the other hand, is in the Old Ghetto Square - Campo Ghetto Vecchio. Before proceeding to the Church of the Madonna of the Garden, a short detour will allow a visit after crossing the Rio S. Girolama, Rio della Sensa and Rio S. Alvise, to the solitary and compact little **CHURCH OF S. ALVISE**. Built in 1388 it has a simple Gothic façade in brick. The only remaining element of the ancient decoration is the statue of St. Alvise above the portal. The in-

1) S. Alvise

2) Church of the Madonna dell'Orto. Façade

3) Church of the Madonna dell'Orto. The presentation of Mary at the Temple (Tintoretto)

4) S. John the Baptist with SS. Peter, Mark, Jerome and Paul (Cima da Conegliano)

terior, with a single nave, contains works of art by Marinali, G. Campagna. A. Zanchi and, among others, two splendid early works by Tiepolo: *The Crowning With Thorns and Flagellation* and the *Way to Calvary*.

Leaving the lovely Campo S. Alvise, returning to the Rio della Sensa along the towpaths (fondamenta) with the same names and going up to the left towards the Rio della Madonna dell'Orto we came to the homonymous church.

THE CHURCH OF **THE MADONNA OF THE GARDEN** (Madonna dell'Orto) was erected towards the middle of the fourteenth century and dedicated to St. Christopher, but it was rebuilt in the XV Century as a votive offering in recognition of a miraculous statue of the Virgin found in a nearby garden. The façade is among the most beautiful in Venice for the transitional characteristics between the Romanesque, Gothic and Renaissance styles. Tripartite with cusped pilaster strips which indicate the positions of the nave and the two aisles in the interior, it is decorated with a crown of small trilobate ogee arches. The *Portal*, with definitely Renaissance characteristics is, however, crowned by an inflected arched gable with decorative elements typical of the decorated Gothic style. It also has three statues: *St. Christopher*, attributed to Raverti, and *St. Gabriel and the Virgin Mary* attributed to A. Rizzo. The five statues representing the *Virgin Mary and the four Evangelists* in the aedicules at the top are all from the eighteenth century. The bell tower is fifteenth century with some elements added in the sixteenth. The *interior*, divided into a nave and two aisles presents elegant sixteenth century decorations recently restored. There are numerous admirable works of art of which we shall mention only a few: *The presentation of the Virgin at the Temple* (1552), *The Last Judgement* (1546), and *The Adoration of the Golden Calf* (1546); all three by Tintoretto. And in addition: *The Madonna and Child* by G. Bellini (1478c), *St. John the Baptist with Saints Peter, Mark, Jerome* *and Paul*, by Cima da Conegliano (1493c).

THE ABBEY OF MERCY (Abbazia della Misericordia) at a short distance from the Church of the Madonna of the Garden, stands in a small, picturesque square. The Abbey Church, dedicated to St. Mary Valverde, was founded in the X Century and restored and altered after long periods of abandonment. The Baroque façade by Clement Moli, with one order of Corinthian pilaster strip was rebuilt in the seventeenth century at the expense of Senator Gaspare Moro.

SANTA FOSCA, near the Rio of the same name, was rebuilt around 1679 on the ruins of the ancient church which preceded it. The façade, of one order with Corinthian pilaster strip is of 1741 while the Gothic bell-tower is XV Century.

From Santa Fosca the *new road* (strada nuova) goes to **ST. SOPHIE** Church on the narrow square of the same name (Campo Santa Sofia) which stretches as far as the Grand Canal. The church has no façade but a bell-tower (which leans considerably) and the interior is divided into a nave and aisles separated by Renaissance style columns. Palma the Younger's *The Depositin of Christ*, should be noted above the side door.

THE **CHURCH OF THE JESUITS**, or Santa Maria Assunta, in the quiet square of the same name, rebuilt on the ruins of the previous church in 1715 to 1730, has a splendid Baroque façade in stone, the work of G. B. Fattoretto (1730c). The interior, a Latin cross with a single nave, is a magnificent embroidery of white and green marbles, gilding, stuccoes, statues and paintings. Among these latter we mention the *Martyrdom of St. Lawrence* by Titian (1558).

The **CHURCH OF THE SAINTS APOSTLES**, built on the site of the previous ancient church and modified in the eighteenth century has a simple brick façade and a bell tower with a somewhat classical bell chamber. The interior which is rectangular in shape has only a nave without aisles and contains, among othes, a beautiful work by Tiepolo: *The*

1) S. Sofia

2) Abbazia della Misericordia

Communion of St. Lucy (1748c).

ST. JOHN CHRYSOSTOM, the last work by Codussi (1497-1504); built on the site of a more ancient church (1080) has a simple Renaissance façade. The interior, in the form of a Greek cross, is considered to be among the finest examples of the Renaissance style in Venice.

The most outstanding works include an altarpiece by S. del Piombo depicting *St. John Chrysostom* with other Saints (1509c) and one of G. Bellini's masterpieces which represents the *Saints Christopher, Jerome and Augustine (1513).*

1) **Jesuit Church**

2) **S. John Chrysostome**

1 ST. SAVIOUR'S - **2** ST. MOISÈ - **3** ST. MARY ZO-BENIGO - **4** ST. STEPHEN'S - **5** ACCADEMIA GALLERY - **6** DELLA SALUTE CHURCH - **7** ST. TROVASO - **8** ST. BARNABAS - **9** CHURCH AND GRAND SCHOOL OF THE CARMINI - **10** ST. SEBASTIAN'S - **11** ST. NICOLÒ OF THE MENDICANTS.

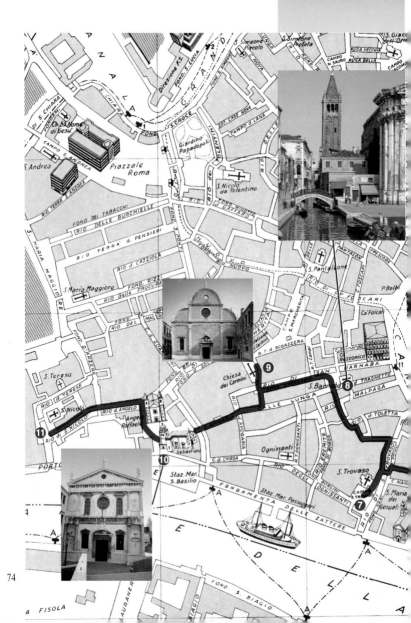

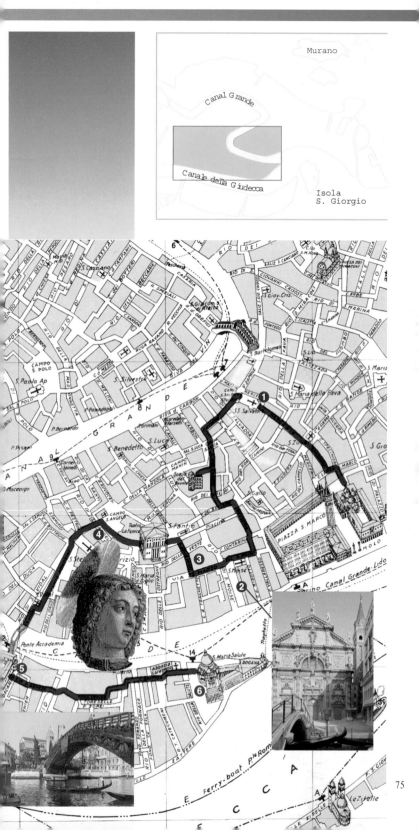

The Church of St. SAVIOUR is reached by walking from St. Mark's Square along Via delle *Mercerie* (Haberdashers), one of the most typical and exciting streets in Venice, lined with innumerable shops. **ST. SAVIOUR'S**, founded in the VII Century, rebuilt in later centuries, owes its present appearance to G. Spavento, to T. Lombardo, and to Sansovino who worked on it in successive phases from 1506 to 1534.

The façade, richly sculptured by B. Falcone was erected in 1663 to a design by G. Sardi. The interior is a notable example of the more mature Renaissance style. Among the more outstanding works of art we must mention a splendid canvas by G. Bellini, the *Supper of Emmaus*; a work by Titian the *Annunciation*, painted in his old age (1566); the statue by Sansovino of *Hope*, looked upon as one of his masterpieces. A short distance away, at the opposite side of *Manin* Square (Campo Manin) in the Calle della Locanda is the **CONTARINI-del BOVOLO PALACE**, famous both for its numerous seventeenth and eighteenth century paintings and for the Renaissance staircase called the SCALA del BOVOLO, the work of G. Candi (1499c). The Palace, which can be visited, is the headquarters of the Municipal Department of Social Assistance. The glorious Renaissance Church of **ST. FANTIN** which was worked on by Scarpagnino and Sansovino (1507 to 1564) is close by. In front of this is the great Venetian theatre LA FENICE, built by Antonio Selva (1790 to 92) in Neoclassical style.

Continuing along the Calle delle Veste we come to the Church of **ST. MOISÈ**, which overlooks Campo San Moisè, with a fine Baroque façade by Tremignon (1668). Founded in the VIII Century, it still has its fourteenth century bell tower. The interior, with a nave without aisles has a fair patrimony of XVII Century and XVIII Century paintings. Worthy of note, among others, is the masterpiece by the Genoese artists N. and S. Roccatagliate (1633), in the sacristy de-

1-2) Palazzo Contarini. Bovolo Staircase

3) La Fenice Theatre. View of the interior before the fire in 1996

picting *Christ carried by Angels, God in Glory and the Pious Women.*

From St. Moisè, along *Calle Larga XXII Marzo* (22nd March) named in memory of the 1848 Revolution, we come to the Church of **ST. MARY OF THE LILY or ZOBENIGO**. The church is named after the Jubanico family which founded it in perhaps the IX Century. Rebuilt in the seventeenth century it has a magnificent Baroque façade by G. Sardi erected between 1678 and 1683 at the expense of the Barbaro family. With a wealth of plastic decoration the façade also has two orders of Ionic and Corinthian semicolumns. The various statues of members of the

1) Church of S. Moisè

2) Palazzo Gritti.
Built in Gothic style, with the characteristic red brick façade. Now a hotel.

3) S. Maria del Giglio or Zobenigo ferry

Barbaro family which adorn the façade include particularly that of Antonio Barbaro, a sea capitan, J. Le Court's last work. The Church has a rectangular nave and interesting works of art including the fine *Abraham divides the World* by A. Zanchi in the Sacristy, and *Four Evangelists* by I. Tintoretto (1552).

Leaving the church to follow Calle Zaguri, Campo S. Maurizio and Calle Spizzler, we arrive eventually at the large square, Campo Morosini, in front of **ST. STEPHEN'S CHURCH**. Built in the fourteenth century, it was modified in the fifteenth and restored at the end of the twentieth century. It is one of the

most beautiful churches in Venice. The simple and elegant Gothic façade is in brick with high one and two-light windows decorated with terracotta cornices. The lovely portal a fine example of decorated Gothic style, is the work of the B. Bon Workshop. The interior is divided into a nave and two aisles by columns in Greek marble and red marble of Verona. The wooden roof in the shape of a ship's keel is very characteristic, as is the use of brick in the walls and the wooden tie-beams which join the walls and the imposts of the arches. The works of art include the *Last Supper, Washing of the Feet*, and the *Sermon in the Garden* by I. Tintoretto and *Madonna and Saints* by Palma the Elder, all in the Sacristy. Another point of interest is the wooden choir, of 1488, carved in Gothic style by M. and F. Cozzi and L. Scalamanzo. There are numbers of sculptured works, some by the Lombardesque school.

ST. SAMUEL'S CHURCH on the square of the same name, Campo S. Samuele, was founded in the XI Century and rebuilt in 1685. It has an interesting XII Century bell tower in Romanesque-Veneto style. The interior has a nave and two aisles and contains among its various works of art, the antique *Ortocosta Virgin*, greatly venerated in the Eastern Empire and brought to Venice by Morea in 1541.

Returning now to Campo Morosini and passing the Corner or Ca' Grande Palace (see itinerary 1.), we cross the Accademia Bridge which leads to the **ACADEMY GALLERIES** (Gallerie dell'Accademia) on the other side of the Grand Canal. The artistic patrimony of these galleries is of primary importance: Venetian painting from the fourteenth to the eighteenth century is documented with numbers of outstanding works. Several polyptyches including the *Virgin Mary, Saints and Prophets* by Lorenzo Veneziano with the works by N. di Pietro which depict *St. Lawrence with the enthroned Madonna and Child and Worshippers* and works by minor artists of the Venetian school, bear testimony to

1) Gallerie dell'Accademia. Lamentation over the Dead Christ - detail (Cima da Conegliano)

2) The legend of S. Ursula - detail (Carpaccio)

3) Entrance to the Gallerie dell'Accademia next to the Scuola della Carità

2

the art of the fourteenth century. The fifteenth century is worthily represented by a most beautiful series of canvasses by Carpaccio which narrate the *Legend of St. Ursula*, the Princess of Britanny executed by the Huns along with 11000 virgins of her country. Other noteworthy fifteenth century works are the *Sacred Conversation* by G. Bellini and the little tablet by Mantegna of *St. George*. The most famous sixteenth century work is the splendid canvas by Giorgione entitled *The Tempest* (1505-7). We must also point out the *Pietà* and *St. John the Baptist* by Titian, Veronese's *Supper in the House of Levi* and the *Miracle of St. Mark*

1) **Gallerie dell'Accademia. S. George - detail (Andrea Mantegna)**

2) **Tempest - detail (Giorgione)**

3) **Portrait of Jacopo Soranzo (Tintoretto)**

1

by Tintoretto. The seventeenth century is documented by Strozzi, Maffei, Mazzoni and others, while the eighteenth, a prolific century, is represented by works by Canaletto, Guardi, the Longhi family, Tiepolo, Rosalba Carriera and Piazzetta. Proceeding in the direction of St. Mark's Basin after leaving the Accademia Galleries, we come to the **DELLA SALUTE CHURCH** (see itinerary 1.) on the last small island between the Grand Canal and the *Giudecca Canal*. Crossing the Rio della Salute, the 8 connected islands which form *Giudecca* can be seen in the distance. In ancient times this was the obligatory residential area of the Jews

1) View of the Basilica della Salute

1

(Giudei) hence its name. it is occupied now mainly by fishermen and manual workers.

Starting once more from the Academia Galleries but in the opposite direction from that to the Della Salute Church, along Calle Pistor, we come to the Church of **ST. TROVASO** after having crossed the Rio named after it. St. Trovaso (a corruption in Venetian dialect of Saints Gervasio and Protasio) stands in the square of the same name – a large, tree-lined, quiet campo. Already in existence in the XI Century, it was rebuilt in Classical form towards the end of the sixteenth century and consacrated in 1657.

The interior in the shape of a Latin cross, contains various works by Tintoretto. The painting of *St. Crisogono on Horseback*, considered a masterpiece of Gothic painting, is attributed to either M. Giambono or I. del Fiore.

Leaving the church by the Calle Toletta and Calle Lotto, we find ourvelves in front of the **CHURCH OF ST. BARNABAS** on Campo S. Barnaba. This eighteenth century church, the work of L. Boschetti, has a fourteenth century brick bell tower.

Continuing along the Fondamenta Gherardini and Calle Pazienza, we come to the Church of ST. MARY OF KARMEL or THE CARMINI and, next to it the

4

SCUOLA GRANDE DEI CARMINI. The *church*, begun in 1286 and consacrated in 1348, is in Gothic style with a Renaissance façade, built in the sixteenth century by S. Mariani da Lugano. It has a nave and two aisles. An altarpiece by Cima da Conegliano depicting *The Nativity with Saints Helena and Catherine, the Guardian Angel and Tobias* (1509c) and a tablet by L. Lotto representing *St. Nicholas between Saints John the Baptist and Lucy and Angels* are among the more important works. The School (La Scuola

Grande), built in the second half of the 17th century and attributed to Longhena is an harmonious classical style edifice which contains a conspicuous collection of Tiepolo's works.

Along the Fondamenta del Soccorso and Fondamenta S. Sebastiano, we arrive at one of the most interesting churches in Venice: the **CHURCH OF ST. SEBASTIAN**, built by Scarpagnini between 1505 and 1548. The church, without aisles, has a façade with two orders of Corinthian columns, is best known for the magnificent collection of works by Paolo Veronese which decorate the interior. They

1) **Scuola dei Carmini and Chiesa dei Carmini**

2) **S. Sebastian's Church**

3) **Church of S. Nicolò**

include: *Hester taken before Ahasuerus, Hester Crowned, The Triumph of Mardocheus*, splendid paintings of from 1555 to 1556, and the great canvas of *Sts. Mark and Marcilian at the Martyrdom comforted by St. Sebastian*, of about 1565.

Leaving St. Sebastian's, and passing the Church of St. Raphael, then Rio S. Nicolò, we follow Fondamenta Lizza Fusina to the **CHURCH OF ST. NICOLÒ OF THE MENDICANTS**. Apparently founded in the VII Century, this is among the most ancient of the Venetian churches and has been restored to its original appearance during the recent restoration.

5 Itinerary

1 CHURCHES OF ST. APONAL - 2 ST. CAS-
SIANO - 3 ST. BOLDO - 4 ST. JAMES dell'ORIO -
5 ST. SIMEONE GRANDE - 6 ST. POLO - 7 BASI-
LICA OF THE FRARI - 8 GRAND SCHOOL OF
ST. ROCCO - 9 THE TOLENTINI.

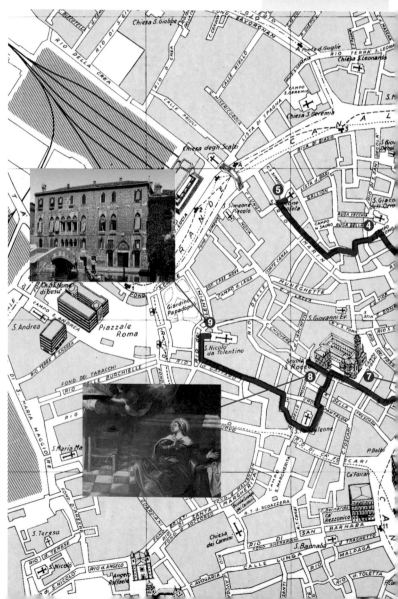

The fifth itinerary, starting from the Church of St. Aponal near the Rialto Bridge, goes in two directions respectively towards the Church of St. Simeone Grande and the Tolentini.

The **CHURCH OF ST. APONAL** or S. Apollinaire, is located in the square or campo of the same name. Founded in the XI Century, then modified in the fifteenth and sixteenth, it has late Gothic character.

A mixed line crowning finishes the façade which has a Renaissance portal decorated with sculptures by A. Rizzo. The interior, with only a nave and flat roof has some fine Renaissance altars and paintings of the seventeenth and eighteenth centuries. These include the altarpiece *The Martyrdom of St. Apollinaire* by L. Querena. To the left of the church, a Romanesque *bell tower* with Gothic restoration, did have one of the most ancient examples of the symbol of Venice: the Lion of St. Mark, with the book closed and wings folded around its head. It is now inside the church.

Leaving the church of St. Aponal and following the labyrinth of lanes, the Calli *del Sole, Sansoni, Rasoi, Muti*, we reach the square or Campo S. Cassiano on which the Church of the same name is located.

The **CHURCH OF ST. CASSIANO**, presumably founded in the X Century, was rebuilt in the seventeenth and some Veneto-Byzantine elements from the ancient church can be seen in the façade. The *bell tower* of the eighteenth century has a XV Century bell chamber. The *interior*, a nave and two aisles, with low cross vaulting, contains works attributed to

1) Characteristic view

2) Rio Marin

3-5) Rio di San Polo

4) S. Giacomo dell'Orio

Tiepolo, Palma the Elder, Tintoretto, and also Bassano, Querena and others. Continuing the itinerary in the direction of the canal, Rio San Boldo, then *Rio Terrà Secondo* and *Calle Tintor*, we come to Campo *S. Giacomo dell'Orio*, a picturesque, treelined square overlooked by council houses. The **CHURCH OF ST. JAMES dell'ORIO** (possibly named after an «alloro» or laurel tree which grew in the vicinity) was founded, it is believed, in the IX Century, rebuilt in 1200, and modified in the XVI Century. The simple white-washed *façade* is decorated with marble fragments from the XII and XIII Centuries. There is an interesting brick bell-tower next to it with a square tower (XII - XIII Century). The different styles of the basilica, harmoniously blended together, can be recognized in the interior in the shape of a Latin cross with a nave and two aisles, a transept and central apse. The wooden roof is in the shape of a ship's keel. Among the numerous important works of art we point out *The Faith* (1577c) by Veronese, in the new sacristy; *The Virgin and Child and Sts. And-*

1) Basilica dei Frari. The apses of the Basilica, seen from Campo S. Rocco

2) Rio dei Frari, the square and the Basilica: an impressive, attractive overall view

3) S. Ambrose Door

4) 15th-century Gothic altar frontal - detail

rew, *James Major, Cosma and Damiano*, by Lorenzo Lotto (1546), in the Presbytery; and two works by Palma the Younger in St. Lorenzo's Chapel: *St. Lawrence aids the Poor* and the *Martyrdom of the Saint*.

Via Campo S. Giacomo, Ruga Bella, Campo S. Sauro, Calle Croce, we go to Rio Marin and skirting this, come out into Campo S. Simeone Grande which faces the Grand Canal. The **CHURCH OF ST. SIMEON the PROPHET**, called S. Simeone Grande, was founded in the X Century and successively altered until it acquired its present appearance with a Neoclassical façade of the middle of the nineteenth century. The interior, with a nave and two aisles, with pointed arches, contains, among others, works by Palma the Younger and Tintoretto: of the former, the *Presentation at the Temple* with portraits of the commissioners, and the *Annunciation*; and *The Last Supper* (1560c) by the latter.

The second branch of our itinerary starting from St. Aponal, along the Calle di Mezzo, the Calle Meloni and Calle della Madoneta, arrives in Campo S. Polo, the largest square in Venice and the theatre of popular festivities in the past. The Campo is framed by the church of the same name, the Corner Mocenigo Palace, Donà Palace, the great Gothic façade of Soanzo Palace, and the Baroque style Tiepolo-Maffetti Palace. The **CHURCH of ST. POLO**, founded it seems, in 737, then rebuilt in Gothic style and frequently altered later, owes its present appearance, Neoclassical, to Davide Rossi who modified it in 1804. Carefully preserved at its side is a large Gothic portal from the Bon workshops and a fourteenth century brick bell-tower. The interior, with a nave and two aisles, still has some elements which were used as a decoration in the restorations, from the fifteenth century construction and from the primitive one. The wooden roof is in the shape of a ship's keel. Among the works of major interest, we mention the *Madonna appears to St. John Nemopuceno*, by G. B. Tiepolo

1-2) Basilica dei Frari. The Madonna di Ca' Pesaro by Titian - details

3) Interior of the Basilica

(1745) and the *Stations on the Via Crucis* by G. D. Tiepolo (1749). Further works are by Palma the Younger, Paolo Veronese, Tintoretto and others. At a short distance from Campo S. Polo, the **BASILICA of the MINOR FRIARS** (known as the Frari) is the church in Venice with the richest collection of works of art after that of St. Mark. It was founded in the middle of the 13th century by the Franciscan Order of Minor Friars, then was rebuilt around 1330 in the present Gothic form and finished towards 1443. Unlike most other examples, it does not have the usual decorative magnificence of the Gothic style, but is an example of rare semplicity and purity. The red colour of the brick walls contrasts with the white of the Istrian stone used for the little aedicules, the capitals, and the other sobre decorations of the portals and the Romanesque bell-tower. The façade in late Gothic style, of simple elegance, is divided into three parts by pilasters surmounted by aedicules with capitals and columns in Veneto-Byzantine style. The upper edge is crowned by a lobate motive, while a brick cornice supported by small pointes arches starts from the façade and continues along the sides of the church. The statues of *Christ Risen*, by Vittoria; of *St. Francis* and of *The Virgin*, by B. Bon are above the pointed arch of the great portal. Three large round windows open in the façade to correspond with the nave and two aisles. The scenery of Campo dei Frari, lapped by the Rio of the same name, which the church faces, has an intimate and quietly composed atmosphere.

The interior of the church, in the shape of a Latin cross, divided into a nave and two aisles, has a warm luminosity. Twelve large pilasters support ogee arches connected by wooden tie-beams. In the middle of the nave, the Choir of the Friars was begun in Gothic style by the Bon workshops and finished in Renaissance style by the Lombardo's in 1475. The 124 stalls inside it, the work of the Cozzi family of carvers of Vicenza are a splendid example of the wood working art in Venice.

The inner façade is decorated at the top with canvasses by Fiorani which represent the *Miracles of St. Anthony* and by a canvas by P. Muttoni which depicts *St. Anthony of Padua and his Basilica.*

On the right of the portal - the monument to Senator Pietro Bernardo, by Tullio Lombardo and, on the left, the monument to the Procurator of St. Mark's Alvise Pasqualigo, attributed to Lorenzo Bregno. The first altar along the left aisle is a 1663 work by Baldassare Longhena. At the second altar a beautiful painting by Giuseppe Porta, called Salviati, represents *The Presentation of the Baby Jesus at the Temple* (1548). At the third altar, a sixteenth century masterpiece by A. Vittoria is the *statue of St. Girolamo* (1565). At the fourth altar is a beautiful altarpiece by Palma the Younger representing the *Martyrdom of St. Catherine.* Worthy of note in the right arm of the transept is the funerary monument to Jacopo Marcello, one of Venice's most beautiful monuments and the work of Pietro Lombardo (XV Century).

Passing now into the Sacristy which houses numerous works of art, we note particularly the *The Madonna and Child Enthroned with Saints*, a triptych by Bellini (1488) which is considered a true masterpiece.

Leaving the sacristy, on the right, we see

the chapel of the Venetian family Bernardo, with a splendid Gothic urn attributed to De Santi or to the Dalle Masegne family. A fine triptych on the altar, representing *The Madonna enthroned with the Child, St. Andrew and St. Nicholas of Bari, St. Paul and St. Peter*, 1482, by Bartolomeo Vivarini, and above, the *Dead Christ.* At the third chapel with an apse, we must point out the wooden statue of *St. John the Baptist* (1438), a masterpiece by Donatello.

In the presbytery, lit in a most effective manner by the great ogee windows, is the most precious treasure of the whole basilica: the *Assumption*, by Titian, a grandiose altarpiece of extraordinary beauty, executed in 1518. On the right of the presbytery we find the monument of Doge Francesco Foscari, in the transitional style between Gothic and Renais-

1) Basilica dei Frari. Triptych by Bellini

2) Wooden choir-stalls in the nave

3-4) Details of polyptych by Bartolomeo Vivarini

5) S. Francis and S. Elizabeth of Hungary - detail (Paolo Veneziano)

sance and, on the left, the great monument to Doge Nicolò Tron, a masterpiece of Renaissance art by Antonio Rizzo.

In the first absidal chapel on the left is a noteworthy altarpiece by Bernardino Licinio which represents the *Madonna and Child and Saints* (1524). In the third chapel, the altarpiece begun by Alvise Vivarini and finished by Basaiti in 1503 represents *St. Ambrose enthroned between Angel musicians and Saints.* In the fourth chapel, a triptych by B. Vivarini depicts *St. Mark enthroned between Angel Musicians and Saints John the Baptist and Gerolamo, Niccolò and Paul.* In the same chapel, the *monument to Federico Corner* is among the most beautiful examples of Venetian Renaissance work (Donnatello school).

Works of note along the left aisles include the *Madonna di Ca' Pesaro*, another excellent work by Titian. And finally the monument to Canova, executed by his followers. On the right side of the basilica are two cloisters of the ex-Convent of the Minor Friars (Frari), called the Ca' Grande which now houses the State Archives.

Next to the Basilica of the Frari, the **GRAND SCHOOL OF ST. ROCCO** (Scuola Grande di San Rocco) faces onto the square of the sama name. Begun in 1515 by Bartolomeo Bon, it was completed by Scarpagnino in 1549. Evidence of the work of both of them can be seen in the façade: the ground floor with elegant two-light windows interspersed with Corinthian columns is by Bon, while the upper level which takes up the motive of Corinthian columns separating double windows, is by Scarpagnino. A competition was held in 1564 for the assignment of the decoration of the interior of the School. All the most famous artists in Venice competed. It was won by Tintoretto who carried out the work over the years 1564 to 1588.

The School still has today an outstanding patrimony of the artist's paintings, the only example of original pictorial decoration still in existence in the Venetian

Schools. Starting from the Hall of the Hotel (Sala dell'Albergo) on the upper floor, then visiting the Great Hall (Salone) on the ground floor, it is possible to study the three successive phases of Tintoretto's work in chronological order. Among his most celebrated works there is *San Rocco in Glory*, with which the artist won the competition, *Christ before*

1) Scuola di S. Rocco. Crucifixion (Tintoretto)

2) School and Church of S. Rocco

3) Upper Hall

4) Annunciation - detail (Tintoretto)

5) Massacre of the Innocents - detail (Tintoretto)

Pilate, Ecce Homo, The Way to Calvary and the magnificently dramatic *Crucifixion*, all part of the first phase of the work.

Memorable works in the Upper Hall include the *Last Supper*, the *Sermon in the Garden*, the *Nativity* the *Resurrection of Lazarus* and other paintings inspired by the Old and New Testaments. Among

4

5

other works in the ground-floor Hall, the *Flight into Egypt* is considered a masterpiece of the artist's later years, and the *annunciation, St. Mary Magdalen* and *St. Mary the Egyptian.* In addition to the numerous works by Tintoretto the School also possesses interesting works by other masters (Titian, G. B. Tiepolo, Zanchi, etc.) and a rich patrimony of objects of art.

From the Grand School of St. Rocco, via the Salizzada S. Pantalon and the Fondamenta Minotto, turning to the right along the Rio dei Tolentini, we arrive at Campo Tolentini where the **CHURCH of** ST. NICOLÒ DA TOLENTINO, built by Scamozzi between 1591 and 1602 is si-

tuated. The eighteenth century façade with a large Corinthian pronaos is the work of Andrea Tirali. The *interior*, inspired according to some, by one of Palladio's models, is in the shape of a Latin cross with only a nave and no aisles, and richly decorated with stuccoes and paintings. Among the works of major interest are the *Annunciation* by Luca Giordano in the presbytery, *St. Lawrence gives the Gold of the Church to the Poor*, and *St. Anthony of Padua* by Strozzi, *Christ in Glory between the Madonna and St. Peter* and *St. Agatha* and *St. Apollonius* by Palma the Younger and *The Annunciation* by Luca Giordano.

The Tolentini Bridge, near the church, leads to the Fondamenta Condulmer and to the Papadopoli Gardens.

The Islands

SAN GIORGIO MAGGIORE - MURANO -
BURANO - S. FRANCESCO NEL DESERTO -
TORCELLO

Sen

Seno della
Seppa

S. Giuliano

M

VENEZIA

Staz^ne
Marittima

Fusina

la Giudecca

S. C

Sacca Sessola

I.S.Spi

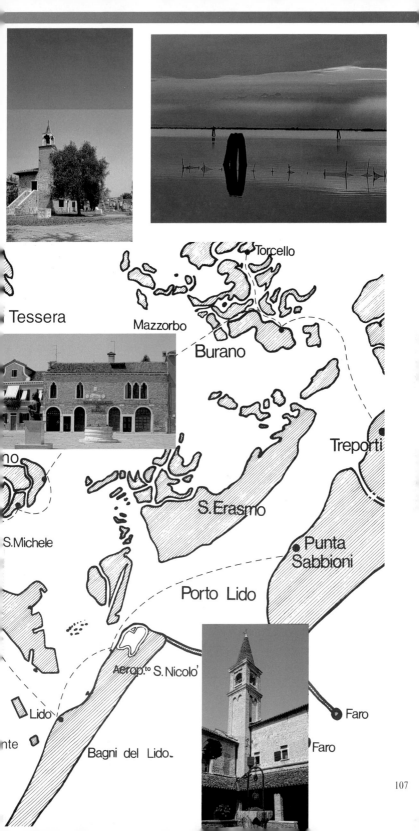

Tessera

Torcello

Mazzorbo

Burano

Treporti

S.Erasmo

S.Michele

Punta
Sabbioni

Porto Lido

Aerop.to S.Nicolo'

Lido

nte

Bagni del Lido

Faro

Faro

107

Numerous islands which can be reached by steamer, are dotted about the tranquil waters of the lagoon between the animated shores of the city and the famous beach of the Lido, overloked by elegant hotels. The Island of ST. GEORGE MAJOR (San Giorgio Maggiore) in St. Mark's Basin is proud of the beautiful

1) Island of S. Giorgio

2) Murano. View of the Church of SS. Mary and Donato

3) Aerial View of Murano

4) Church of SS. Mary and Donato. View of the nave

5) Burano. The unmistakeable crooked spire is a local landmark

façade of the Palladian Church. MU-RANO, the famous for its glass working craftmanship, is a Venice in miniature. BURANO, colourful and evocative, produces famous laces. Quiet reigns at ST FRANCIS in the DESERT (S. Francesco nel Deserto), a Franciscan centre of prayer, and the TORCELLO, the original nucleus of Venice. This and many other islands are worthy of a visit in the fascinating lagoon scenery.

1) Torcello. Aerial view of the Basilica

2) Torcello. The Church of S. Fosca

3) S. Francesco del Deserto. Overall view towards Burano and the North Lagoon.

Text: Lucia Colonna
Translation: A.B.A. - Milan
Printed by: Kina Italia S.p.A. - Milan